SELECTED POEMS

JAMES REEVES

SELECTED POEMS

edited and introduced by
John Howlett

Greenwich Exchange
London

Greenwich Exchange, London

First published in Great Britain in 2021
All rights reserved

Selected Poems
© the estate of James Reeves, 2021

Introduction © John Howlett
Foreword © Gareth Reeves

This book is sold subject to the conditions that it shall not, by way of trade or otherwise, be lent, resold, hired out or otherwise circulated without the publisher's prior consent in any form of binding or cover other than that in which it is published and without a similar condition including this condition being imposed on the subsequent purchaser.

Printed and bound by imprintdigital.com
Cover design by December Publications
Tel: 07951511275

Greenwich Exchange Website: www.greenex.co.uk

Cataloguing in Publication Data is available from the British Library

ISBN: 978-1-910996-53-9

CONTENTS

Gareth Reeves: Foreword *13*

John Howlett
   Intense Silence: The Poetry of James Reeves *17*

from THE NATURAL NEED (1936)

Hartland Quay *37*

Repose *38*

At the Window *39*

Winter Speculation *40*

Thoughts and Memories *41*

from THE IMPRISONED SEA (1949)

The Dancers *45*

The Conspirators 1940 *46*

Bestiary *47*

Misgivings *48*

Greenhallows *49*

Aeons Hence *52*

Music in the Wood *53*

For Years We Traced *54*

Two Minds *55*

Thoughts Indoors *56*

A Matter of Discipline *57*

from THE PASSWORD (1952)

The Tree of Life *61*

A Violin Concerto *62*

Had I Passion to Match my Skill *63*

Leaving Town *64*

In the Train *65*

In the Clubhouse *66*

The Prisoners *67*

A Fire I Lit *68*

The Little Brother *69*

Old Crabbed Men *70*

Fragments of a Landscape *71*

Vulture Absence *72*

A Sonnet in Winter *73*

Novels I Have Never Written *74*

The Infernal Machine *76*

The Stone Gentleman *77*

Counsel to Boys *78*

'A Letter to Posterity' *79*

Poet of Birds *80*

from THE TALKING SKULL (1958)

To Norman Cameron 1905-1953 *83*

This Mood of Murder *84*

'And So They Came to Live at Daffodil Water' *85*

On a Poet *86*

The Talk *87*

An Academic *88*

Homage to the Moth *89*

from THE QUESTIONING TIGER (1964)

Evolution of a Painter *93*

Important Insects *94*

De Fesch *95*

A Stoical Robin *96*

Discharged from Hospital *98*

No Tears for Miss Macassar *99*

Demigods *100*

Generation of a Critic *101*

Bruges *102*

The Tiger *103*

Planning Permission *104*

Poor Woman *106*

Improvisations *107*

Indirect Speech *109*

Goat and Compasses *110*

The Solvers *111*

Grand Opera *112*

from SUBSONG (1969)

All Days but One *115*

This Corrupt Music *116*

Song (The Sleep I Lost) *117*

Metamorphosis *118*

The Meeting *119*

A Sonata by Handel *121*

Faces at the Brink *122*

No Strawberries from Mr Wright *123*

You and Not You *125*

Personality Cult *126*

Poetry Festival *127*

On Two Poets *128*

The Battle of Lewes: 14 May 1264 *129*

from POEMS AND PARAPHRASES (1972)

Rough Weather *133*

Not To Be Greedy *134*

The Spark *135*

Late Love *136*

September Dusk *137*

Message *138*

The Children *139*

Fin De Saison *140*

Animula *141*

from THE CLOSED DOOR (1977)

Madrigal *145*

The Closed Door *146*

The Marriage of Figaro *147*

The Act of Death *149*

References

A Note on the Text

Acknowledgments

Index of Titles

FOREWORD

IN THIS EXCELLENT SELECTION JOHN HOWLETT makes a serious case for the poetry of my father as 'deeply philosophical', a quietly reasonable 'subsong' (the title of one of his collections). I was aware that when my dad climbed the stairs to his study to earn the family's living, it was a demanding business. He was extraordinarily stoical in his daily routine as a freelance writer: in spite of near blindness his rate of production was prodigious, as critic, educationist, editor, folk song specialist, as well as poet. His poems for children continue to be read the world over: in this area he is an international star. So it is gratifying to see this selection correct the balance in favour of the unjustly neglected adult poetry. But perhaps inevitably it was his children's poetry that first made me aware my dad wrote poetry at all. It strikes me now, though, how often the children's poetry can be a comic reflection of the 'grown-up'. His presence about the house was like that too: upstairs he could be heard nearsightedly bashing away at the typewriter (sometimes getting his fingers on the wrong keys and unwittingly rattling off a coded message), but downstairs he was convivial, enjoyed company, gave frequent dinner parties (after my mother's untimely death he liked to do the cooking with the aid of a magnifying glass), and enjoyed pronouncing judgement on so-and-so and such-and-such. As man and writer he really liked a laugh, and the children's poems are often very funny, sometimes quite tartly so. The first poem by my dad that I learnt by heart was 'W'. It is still one of my favourite squibs for kids:

> The King sent for his wise men all
>   To find a rhyme for W;
> When they had thought a good long time
> But could not think of a single rhyme,
>   'I'm sorry,' said he, 'to trouble you.'

And here is an adult squib:

> Be Certain, Mr A to Z,
>   That when the vulture drops its dirt
> Upon your undistinguished head
>   It is not chance but your desert.

The targets are similar: 'important insects', to quote another poem. But the first is wry, the second savage (the particular target is Alvarez). Both are written with a characteristically undemonstrative and unpretentious skill. My father couldn't abide pretentiousness, which, with a bit of straining, might be said to be the target of this quatrain from the children's book *Prefabulous Animiles*, but here the tone is pure delight:

> The Nonny-bird I love particularly;
>   All day she chirps her joysome odes.
> She rises perpendicularly,
>   And if she goes too far, explodes.

– with a 'joysome' illustration of the exploding bird by my

father's friend and long-time collaborator, the portly Edward Ardizzone, who, with his wife, used to visit us in their bubble car, and would chuckle when I sneezed after pleading to sniff the snuff he always had with him. On the other hand my father was partial to cigars, which he smoked late into the night over a whisky nightcap. Once he fell asleep mid-smoke and set the living room on fire; his library and LP record collection were kippered.

Over the years, inevitably differences between father and son began to emerge, though I realise now that many of these were inseparable from the paternal influence. After all, how many sons can say that they would argue with their father about the merits of Brahms, whose chamber music is in my opinion out of this world but was dismissed by my dad out of hand (or so I thought until I realised he'd done his homework, when, many years later, I came across a box of old Brahms LP-78s in the attic), or would have to swallow his disapproval when I chose as a school prize the collected poems of Dylan Thomas? The point is that without my father's influence perhaps I never would have got excited about classical music, or poetry, or lots of other things (woodwork for instance). At any rate, for better or for worse I seem to have inherited the poetry thing, and after my father's death I wrote a sequence of poems called *Going Blind*, which circle around various objects he owned and have ended up in our house. One poem began life while I was contemplating his clutch of walking sticks. It seems to echo Marquez's ruminations, in *Love in the Time of Cholera*, about 'sons whom life has turned, little by little, into the fathers of their fathers':

Tentacles

Over the years my hand ended up
in the downward position
and he wasn't tugging, but being tugged.

This wouldn't do. Gradually
I was guiding him by the elbow,
but only at critical junctures

and at exactly the right speed,
his other hand holding his stick,
an extended arm, feeling, inching ...

Our eight limbs went spidering
over the web of the pavement.

Be that as it may, this selection and John's introduction do a great job of demonstrating, to quote the title of one my father's many books, his 'commitment to poetry'.

Gareth Reeves

INTENSE SILENCE:
THE POETRY OF JAMES REEVES

AS WITH HIS CLOSE FRIEND AND onetime mentor Robert Graves, the life and literary achievements of James Reeves (1909-1978) recall a much earlier time and place. His Stakhanovite work ethic – writing, editing, overseeing and compiling over 100 books which encompassed not just poetry but also novels, children's literature, folk song texts, academic works, pedagogic guides, as well as a number of critical editions – is redolent of the Victorian age replete with its dense 'three-deckers' and men-of-letters who traversed with ease a range of academic forms and genres. Further to that, his poetry (the focus here) happily sidestepped many of the passing trends of the twentieth century. One will struggle in the pages of Reeves to find poems which resonate with the prevailing fashions of the day, compete with the more abstruse trend-setters or make any sort of direct comment on contemporary events such as the Second World War. There is no politics in Reeves and his tastes – Clare, Hardy, Thomas Gray – were very often orthodox. As such, his poetry has been difficult to classify, which has led both to a wide misunderstanding as to its importance, but also a tendency to downplay and disregard its sparkling originality. Even the reverential terms of an official obituary could only damn Reeves with faint praise: 'His poems had all of the virtues and none of the vices of Georgian poetry' (*The Times*, 9 May 1978). It is hard, on reading his body of work over forty years on, to see any veracity in such claims.

Perhaps this tendency to misalign Reeves aids in explaining why a number of his poems became staples of anthologies, for both adults and children. Indeed, he was one of a very small number of 'serious' poets to write equally successfully for the young; in recent times only Walter de la Mare, Hilaire Belloc and maybe Roy Fuller have come close to matching his skill in this regard. Being however difficult to pin down would not, one feels, have greatly bothered him. Following Graves, his understanding of the nature of poetry derived from what he saw as the need to capture the intensity of localised experience. This was not fidelity toward a Muse or Goddess figure but instead writing 'rooted in the particular and the immediate' (Reeves, 1960, 15). For Reeves, poems were a product of 'psychic disturbance' (ibid, 11), a state characterised 'neither of extreme happiness nor of extreme misery' and where 'the poet is acutely conscious of himself and his feelings, not as self and feelings, but as language' (ibid, 12). Whereas adherence to similar precepts led Graves to occasional bombast and to dismiss poets not so inspired (he never for example thought much of, amongst others, W.H. Auden or Dylan Thomas), Reeves' life by contrast was lived in a far quieter, although no less concentrated, register and his wholehearted commitment to the cause and value of poetry was summed up in one of his most reflective lyrics: 'Be absolute for poetry, my friend,/Or your insatiate spirit will go hungry,/Knocking on deaf men's doors to ask for bread' ('Message', lines 1-3). Such hunger was to be equally well satiated in his adroit, fair, and skilful criticism as well as his frequent advocacy of the craft particularly amongst children and as it was taught in schools. This was, after all, a man who revelled in living with, 'The taste of salt for ever on my tongue' (ibid, line 12).

Paying tribute to another of his many friends, Edmund Blunden, Reeves was moved to observe that, 'Having no Celtic bombast in his blood,/Nor dipsomaniac rage, nor very much/ To give his time of what his time expected,/He saw his Muse, slight thing, by most neglected' ('On a Poet', lines 1-4). In the years since, Blunden has rightly won his laurels, yet the sentiments here ascribed seem now more appropriate to their author than to their subject. Whereas other poets championed by Graves such as Norman Cameron (2011), Martin Seymour-Smith (2006) and Alun Lewis (2008) have had welcome reclamations, Reeves, despite his prolific output, has remained comparatively forgotten. Aside from a recent re-issuing of his children's poems (2009) – none of which therefore need be included here – and a short pamphlet compiled by Robert Nye (2009) which contained only 17 poems, those wishing to read Reeves' work in bulk would have had to trawl for the long out of print *Collected Poems 1929-1974* which was published towards the end of his life and included most of the poems from his published volumes as well as two uncollected pieces.

Such a comparative slide into anonymity can be attributed, in part at least, to the treatment afforded to Reeves by W.B. Yeats who refused him entry into his *Oxford Book of Modern Verse* on the grounds that he was 'too reasonable, too truthful', the Muses apparently preferring 'gay warty lads'. Yeats' slightly idiosyncratic selection also infamously omitted Wilfred Owen and the War Poets, the best new work of

Macspaunday and his brilliant Irish contemporary Austin Clarke and should therefore be easy to discount but for the fact that such an attitude appears to have lingered. The more recent *Oxford Companion to Modern Poetry in English*, for example, referred to a 'general lack of passion or even character' (Hamilton 1996, 447) in Reeves' writing whilst Peter Scupham, in one of the rare extended treatments given to him, explains that: 'Reeves is still valued by a few, but remains largely unconsidered, unacknowledged, undiscussed' (Scupham 2000, 40). This assessment holds true twenty years later with only one short article appearing in any academic journals (see Politis 2012) and a general absence of any broader scholarship. Rarely has a poet so prolific been so poorly served. Furthermore, Reeves has suffered through association; as a protest against his earlier exclusion by Yeats, the ever-loyal Laura Riding, who thought highly of her young protégé, withdrew her own anthology contribution thereby adding to the mythology of a protected 'Graves circle' and subsuming Reeves within this group, which also included other forgotten and less talented poets such as Alan Hodge and Geoffrey Taylor. It is to be hoped then that this present selection goes some way toward righting these wrongs and reinstating Reeves as a poet not just of great skill but also of intellect, wit, compassion, and inventiveness.

James Reeves was born John Morris Reeves at Harrow-on-the-Hill in 1909 to Alfred John Reeves, a company secretary, and his wife Ethel Mary. His parents were of northern Methodist origin and were somewhat puritan in outlook, inculcating a prudish streak their youngest son was to never quite lose. Following his prep schooling at Nevill House, Eastbourne he was one of the earliest students to attend the newly-formed Stowe School in Buckinghamshire going up as their first Top Entrance Scholar in 1923. The affection he had for his *alma mater* is suggested by a longstanding correspondence with his headmaster, the charismatic J.F. Roxburgh, which continued into the 1950s, copies of which are in the school archive. Having acquired a Higher Certificate (French and English) Reeves subsequently went up to Jesus College, Cambridge armed with an open scholarship to study what today is known as Modern Languages. In an introductory letter to the College's Master, Reeves was described as having a 'good deal of literary gift, and [as] the sort of man who runs a School Magazine and a Debating Society with enterprise' although it was noted that he was 'in himself a perfectly sound and nice fellow though in no way a leader' (Letter from J.F. Roxburgh to the Master of Jesus College, Stowe School archives, 5 November 1927). At Jesus, Reeves studied under the Elizabethan scholar E.M.W. Tillyard, emerging with an upper second degree in both parts of the tripos.

Of greater significance than his formal studies, however, were the ways in which Cambridge provided, as it had always done for those so gifted, a space for Reeves to fully develop his budding literary abilities. Oxford may have claimed Auden and his followers but 'the Other Place' was no less abundant with talent and, surrounded by a coterie that included Jacob Bronowski, Michael Redgrave and Alastair Cooke, Reeves was part of a particularly closely-knit group that founded the literary magazine *Experiment* which ran for three years from 1928-1931, and of which Bronowski and Hugh Sykes Davies were editors. The attitude of the journal as expressed in its first issue was one of 'uncompromising independence' and with a desire amongst its authors to not be 'littered with the Illustrious Dead and Dying' (*Experiment* Number 1, 1928, 1). Bullishness of this kind amongst young men is perhaps to be expected and, as is the case with many similar undergraduate magazines and anthologies, the contents rarely lived up to such lofty goals and were often uneven and lacking authorial maturity. However, for all that is lacking, such publications do still serve to provide a snapshot of the networks, groupings and prevailing *zeitgeist* of an exact time and place. In this case we see the first published poems of another precocious contemporary, William Empson, as well as a number of contributions from Kathleen Raine and the future Arthurian novelist T.H. White. Reeves may not have known them all, nor always kept in touch in later life, but their presence nevertheless indicates something of the circles in which he moved and the direct literary influences upon the up-and-coming writer. He himself also had a number of poems published in the magazine and whilst not all were successful or memorable – he was still one of *those* young men after all! – several were to be incorporated into his own first collection.

Having graduated in 1931, and like so many of his generation from similar backgrounds (Betjeman, Day-Lewis, Auden), Reeves began a career in teaching, first at Holloway School (1933-1935) then, later, at Slough Grammar School (early 1940s-1947), Weymouth Teacher Training College (1947-1953) and finally at St Edmund's School, Canterbury. His classroom methods can be gleaned from a reading of some of his later pedagogic works, in particular *Teaching Poetry* (1958) which put forward the view that, 'poetry should be so taught that a poem is the centre of an active and pleasurable experience, not a text in black and white on the page of a book; the poetry lesson should be lively, and methods should be constantly varied' (Reeves 1958, 28). This involved ensuring children were given opportunities to write their own poems ('rough, vigorous, lively, possibly ungrammatical and unrhythmical verse' (ibid, 92)) as well as being made to think about how poetry intersected with other art forms like drama and art. In light of progressive developments from the 1960s onwards around the teaching of English, it is clear that Reeves' thinking was influential upon his profession and pointed the way toward later curriculum changes which begun to stress the importance of children's self-expression. Moreover, his justification for the studying of poetry (and the arts in general) was that it allowed – democratically and without any hint of instrumentalism – for a degree of individual fulfilment and this perhaps explains why he was much liked and respected by his students.

Progressively failing eyesight – the reason for the termination of his first teaching post – meant however that he was forced prematurely to retire from his chosen profession, moving to Chalfont St Giles in Buckinghamshire where out of necessity he became an industrious freelance writer relying on this income to support his wife and young family. Those years in the classroom had however not seen any diminution of his earlier literary activity or ambition and, having earlier sent his poems for comment to Robert Graves and Laura Riding, was rewarded by an invitation to visit them in Mallorca, an offer he finally accepted in 1935. Described by Miranda Seymour as 'Small, moustachioed and pipe-smoking' Reeves at the time 'projected an air of remoteness that was increased by the thick spectacles which hid his eyes'

(Seymour, 1995, 231). This first visit entailed him not only entertaining the locals by singing folk songs and ballads accompanied by his guitar (he also played the piano and was a more than competent performer) but also contributing to the Graves/Riding volume *Epilogue I* as well as compiling his early poems for publication. This relationship was to be the most important of Reeves' literary life and marked too the start of Graves' devout loyalty to his newly-acquired friend's poetry. As he was to outline to Edward Marsh: 'His name is James Reeves, he is about twenty-eight, Cambridge, schoolmastering somewhere, and the poems will appear as a Seizin Press book this autumn and you shall have a copy. It is so many years that there has been a good new poet, that it is worth a jubilee' (Robert Graves to Edward Marsh, 12 May 1935, quoted in O'Prey 1982, 245).

The volume referred to here, which Graves initially printed at his own expense before attracting a mainstream publisher, was entitled *The Natural Need* and, as we have mentioned, it incorporated some of Reeves' undergraduate work as well as a number of new poems. Nevertheless, despite its patron's vigorous championing, in hindsight, and like many debut collections, we can see it as a poet searching to establish a distinctive identity and therefore not being altogether successful. This possibly explains why only eight poems from its twenty-seven were selected when their author came later in life to collect his work. Undoubtedly there are some good pieces but, unlike his mature writing, several of the poems are too long (Reeves was usually always better in a shorter, more concise mode) and the influences of his contemporaries are too obviously felt. Many of the voices here are those of imitation and the work is weaker for it. Laura Riding in her introductory preface-poem to *The Natural Need* in fact cautioned that, 'The ways to that late habit of speech/[Which] is a wisdom-time of nature' and in the case of Reeves the 'wisdom-time' would entail a gap of thirteen years before the appearance of a second volume, *The Imprisoned Sea*. Such a lengthy period, much of it spent in the classroom, had however allowed him to shed any youthful derivation and, unencumbered now by his student voice, this work signalled the emergence of the true Reeves in which his characteristic tone and register were established and the mastery of speech rhythms, whether in freer forms or more formal stanzas, was apparent. Indeed, Robert Nye has gone as far to say that he felt this to be the strongest of Reeves' collections and fine poems such as 'Greenhallows', 'Bestiary' and 'Thoughts Indoors' add weight to this claim.

As a now full-time writer Reeves rapidly emerged not merely as a poet in his own right – there were to be six further collections in the next eighteen years bringing the total number of individual poems to over 250 – but also a pre-eminent anthologist and editor. Serving as general editor of William Heinemann's *Poetry Bookshelf* series from 1951, he oversaw the publication of scholarly editions of most of the established canon, even producing a number himself including Clare, Donne, Chaucer and Hopkins, works which give us a further clue as to his own passions and identification with a particular strand of English poetry. Other contributors to the series included fellow poets Donald Davie, John Heath-Stubbs and G.S. Fraser, suggesting the wide range of friendships that the ever-sociable Reeves was wont to cultivate. Many of these also submitted poems to *Quarto* which was a poetic broadsheet edited by Reeves and which ran throughout 1951 and 1952. Around this time Reeves was also appointed general editor of Unicorn Books, a children's publisher which overlapped with his emerging output of children's verse. Beginning with *The Wandering Moon* in 1950, he produced a number of collections for children as well as various stories and novels, many of which were distinctively illustrated by Edward Ardizzone in a partnership that sustained for over twenty years. Perhaps Reeves saw his children's writing as a way to compensate for the poor diet of poems young children were habitually fed in school.

Of most interest however, and beginning with *The Poets' World* (1948), were his critical works which showed something of Reeves' view of the role of the poet, and one which rejected the more obviously elitist Romantic position: 'a true poet resents being thought peculiar and 'different'. He would prefer to be thought of as a man in the fullest sense, but withdrawn from the rest of the world by a capacity, partly innate and partly trained, to speak to others, and by recognition of the responsibilities which this entails' (Reeves 1965, 42). Such a description could fairly be applied to Reeves himself. Stemming from these rapidly-forming convictions, his wider poetic opinions, although always scholarly and considered, were occasionally waspish and he was unafraid to cull sacred cows where he felt they deviated from the characteristics he most admired. Sentimentality ('one of the commonest causes of bad poetry ... When we are sentimental we are ... pretending we feel deeply about something we cannot really feel at all' (Reeves 1956, 80)) as well as flamboyance and ostentatiousness ('Rhetorical and showy verse is always something to be regarded with suspicion' (ibid, 129)) were for him the cardinal sins of any writer. On those grounds, and as a riposte to orthodox interpretation, he championed a number of lesser-known poets including Hartley Coleridge, Fulke Greville and Trumbull Stickney.

The principle virtue of many of those he admired was *directness* and this explains why his re-imagining of the canon also gave primacy to folk song and balladry, an area of study he has been given scant recognition for helping to revive. Indeed, his most obviously scholarly books, *The Idiom of the People* (1958) and *The Everlasting Circle* (1960), showcased traditional folk song and drew upon the manuscripts of Cecil Sharp as well as those of other collectors like Sabine Baring-Gould, H.E.D. Hammond, and George B. Gardner. In these, Reeves sought to rescue and reprint the original versions of the songs they had gathered as many had previously been bowdlerised – a result of prissy late Victorian sensibilities. Often, the original versions were far more earthy and it is typical of Reeves' commitment to a primitive 'man of the people' form of honesty that these were printed unexpurgated: 'Without being subtle or refined in form, it [folk song] appeals directly to the common man or woman in each of us ... It expresses true feeling, without sentimentality or sensationalism ... folk song is often the expression of the spirit of rebellion and non-acceptance of the repressive standards of respectable society' (Reeves 1965, 64).

Towards the end of his life Reeves moved to the quiet Sussex town of Lewes where, despite being almost blind and relying on local sixth-formers to read to him, he continued his copious writing and editing. He also contributed to the intellectual life of the local area, writing various verse dramas for schools to perform and setting up a chamber music society. Belatedly, he was elected a Fellow of the Royal Society of

Literature in 1976 and a last small pamphlet of poems appeared in the year before his death. His wife having died in 1966 meant that these were not however always happy times and many of the poems from his last decade carry as their theme meditations of sadness and absence. As he put it, 'But now evening descends, the leaves descend,/And yawning waiters hurry on my death' ('Fin de Saison', lines 3-4). Reeves did not have long to wait: he died on 1 May 1978 and was buried with his wife in the local cemetery down the road. His simple headstone, in many ways so characteristic of the man, recalls nothing but his name and dates.

In coming now to read and appraise Reeves it is inevitable that the preconceptions surrounding his work will cast shadows. The popular view of him – admittedly one often held by those who have not read him properly if at all – as a neo- or even post- Georgian means that unavoidably his work is seen at first glance under that damning aspect. However, as a reading of the contents in this book will hopefully demonstrate, the very characteristics one expects to find in Reeves – gentle, pastoral, detached – are marked more by their absence and rarely does he exhibit the worst faults he identified in his predecessors, notably 'imprecise diction and facile rhythm; sentimentality of outlook [and] downright commonplace themes' (Reeves 1962, xvii). In fact, as Robert Nye has pointed out, 'there was always another Reeves, a Reeves who wrote unpredictable, erotically-inspired, rather angry poems that welled up from a much more peculiar source' (Nye 2009, 1). Whilst it could be argued that 'erotically-inspired' is too strong and over-egged, there was nonetheless undeniably more bite to Reeves than has previously been acknowledged. One such of his moods was satirical and in poems such as 'The Meeting', 'Indirect Speech' and the very funny when read aloud 'Planning Permission' we find him railing gently against bureaucracy and the opaque language of officialdom. In a similar vein, rarely has his own profession been as succinctly skewered as in 'Generation of a Critic' in which 'The tongue is shrill, the ink turned poison,/ Getting and keeping you in print' ('Generation of a Critic', lines 15-16) whilst elsewhere he neatly takes to task those who negate serious consideration of their subject for the sake of gossip ('Personality Cult').

More generally however, and fitting for someone who so distrusted cant and had no time for hypocrisy, other poems move to question the idea of authority in a broader sense. Witness for instance, 'How troublesome the mammoths of the world,/Gross and assertive' ('Bestiary' lines 15-16) or else, 'Despite their busy, devious trafficking/Important insects simply do not matter' ('Important Insects', lines 13-14). We may today take issue with the occasional schoolmasterly tone but Reeves finds his targets. Such attacks did not though mean that Reeves was, in any sense, anti-establishment and in fact he appeared to know all too well the lesson of contrarian opposition: 'Rebels beneath the banners of dissent:/You'll live to see them man no barricades/But climb the pulpits of the establishment' ('On Two Poets', lines 3-4). In thus embodying Robert Frost's aphorism about refusing to be radical when young so as not to later become conservative Reeves sat precariously in the middle, somewhere 'in the interstices/Of a declining age' ('Bestiary' lines 17-18). Perhaps for him – a man in whose work any politics might loosely be termed *social politics* – it was not desirable to usurp but, rather, better to push to one side as in the case of his 'Stone Gentleman' who, having too long been unwelcome, is shuffled off where, 'Unchallenged and without affront [he] shall manage/The republic of tall spiders' ('The Stone Gentleman', lines 11-12). Reeves' poetry therefore calls for a gentler, less dogmatic way of musing upon the world and a central feature of his work is his ability to make us raise a proverbial eyebrow to the familiar. In this one is maybe reminded both of Norman Maccaig, with whom temperamentally Reeves shares similarities, but more so his beloved Hardy who had an equally impressive gift for reflecting on the commonplace and the poet's place within it. Poems such as 'Grand Opera', 'The Marriage of Figaro' and 'A Sonata by Handel' for instance contain or end with questions and invite us, albeit in his own tight-lipped and valedictory way, to consider the relationship between art and memory but also the extent to which art, in this case music, can ever be imitative of real life. The fact that such speculations – found too in 'The Prisoners' – echo ancient concerns of Plato, his Forms and the Allegory of the Cave only substantiates the point that Reeves' work is always deeply philosophical, albeit with its learning lightly worn. This desire to provoke questions as much as to provide answers is also found in a number of poems where Reeves turns the critical gaze inward. On occasion as in 'A Stoical Robin' – 'mine/Remains imprisoned in my feebleness' ('A Stoical Robin, lines 31-32) – or else 'Had I Passion to Match my Skill' these musings lead him almost to the point of self-loathing, but these are not confessional cravings for attention. Rather, they represent ruminations on the nature of inspiration and limitations of the poet's craft. 'Novels I Have Never Written' for example is a stream of consciousness trot through plots, characters and archetypes (if only they *had* been written!) in which Reeves himself emerges as the 'disconsolate hero' ('Novels I Have Never Written', line 20). Better still, 'And so they Came to Live at Daffodil Water', a phrase conjured to the poet's mind (Scupham here sees John Crowe Ransom but this could easily be a Wordsworthian *melange*), sparks a brief meditation and then is gone with only questions remaining as to who the titular *they* were and why they would want to come at all. Neither the voice that implanted the phrase nor aspirations toward locating it in a bigger canvas can be met.

Such disconnected visions reach their zenith in 'Greenhallows', a more obviously complex poem, but one which also introduces that ability of Reeves to unsettle and disturb. Having travelled in a manner befitting Auden (note 'The wires saluted me', line 7) to a stately home containing paintings of his own choosing and with a visitors' book full of his own signatures, the poem's narrator is eventually transported out of this nightmarish setting to something approximating the real world: 'I need not tell you how I ran,/ My chaplet fallen, my toga disarrayed./I noticed the door was marked 'Out Patients'/And a man in a white coat raged and flapped.' ('Greenhallows', lines 77-80). Whilst serving as an attack on hubris, the poem's surreal inter-weavings masterfully exemplify those notes of anxiety and caution. His nightmare has suddenly become ours. The space between certainties was clearly a difficult one to occupy and, elsewhere, poems like 'Winter Speculation', 'The Dancers' or 'For Years We Traced' find visions of half-remembered utopias and arcadias which are seen through the corrupting prism of experience and are often interrupted: 'Too late he saw the watcher in the shade/Signal from the laurels beside the lawn,/

The circle close and the love figure vanish/In a maze of pointed feet, a flash of hair.' ('The Dancers', lines 1-4).

In creating fragments of narrative, such works drill down to the very essence of Reeves as a poet whose form in many ways was *small* and *local*; he wrote only a handful of long poems and thus it is quite possible to read most of his work in one sitting. Similarly, he found it impossible to ever address the events and times in which he lived. What could only be understood through other media (newspapers, films, the radio) could not, he believed, be articulated on the page. What is therefore presented to us are little shards of a man's mind and imagination. This is not to say however that we should always mistake any laconic detachment as a substitute for more worldly engagement or that it is not possible to somehow gather the poems together to produce a cohesive whole. In this task we are aided by Reeves who, in his introduction to the late volume *Subsong* (1969), adumbrated something of his own poetic creed. Borrowing from the ornithologist D.W. Snow, the titular subsong was a term used to denote birdsong which, 'differs chiefly from subdued song and full autumn song in being much quieter, only audible a few yards away ... "for the sole benefit of the performer" ... it has a certain ventriloquial quality and is frequently given from thick cover, so that the singer, though only a few feet away, is often very difficult to locate' (Reeves 1969, vii). The notes of this song and its peculiar spirit are felt more obviously in the later volumes, yet it seems unlikely that the ever-reflective Reeves was unaware that this tune had been sung for him before. On the fringes of the Cambridge avant-garde, part of the Graves circle, but not embracing their wild flights of fancy, never one swept along by popular fashions, he had always been a closeted observer and narrator of his own and others' behaviour.

Reeves' best work has then much in common with the spirit of the folk songs he so loved; it is direct, free of padding, it speaks justly and straightforwardly and the voice is truthful. It is above all honest and an antidote to a time 'Where every poet is a megaphone/Which shouts immortal megaphone' ('Poetry Festival', lines 3-4). It is a poetry whose voice is quiet and subdued yet which does not proselytise; whose writer is sharply observant but who does not seek to make grand claims for or about you. Over-sophistication was to be feared and, in lines that should still resonate today, 'The nightmare of sensationalism, violence, hysteria and threatened destruction ... removes all relevance and meaning from the only kind of poetry I can write' (Reeves, 1960, 15). Above all though it is a body of work – and a life – dedicated to Eliot's precept that there was not enough silence in the world. For too long the voice has been undetectable; it is time now for it to be heard.

John Howlett

from
The Natural Need
(1936)

HARTLAND QUAY

Go to the sea, then. Pack a bag and stay
Long enough to know the times of posts
And where to bathe and when, and to get brown.
Go and climb the inland-tilted cliffs
And scale the rocks that overhang the sea.
Pursue the glittering snailtrack over lichen
On hands and feet, and from the stony face
Chip crystals with the ferrule of your stick.

You'll turn your back on the indifferent sea,
View it no longer, let your ears reject
The gulls' falsetto, siren to your aim,
Leave spongy coombs and shallow rockpools, paths
That tempt you up to crests of gaudy ling,
Forget the cry of sunlight and salt wind,
The fragile bones of seabirds on the cliff
Forget such things, and since your blood responds
To the incessant wheedling of the sea,
Forget it too. Leave it for those not made
To stand in danger from its sorceries.

You are safer travelling homewards in a train,
Reading the paper, meeting other people
And eyes of friends, hurtful but undeceiving.
Deny the sea, the flattery of birds,
And starve corrupting elements from your blood.

REPOSE

Repose is in simplicities.
Perhaps the mind has leaves like trees,
Luxuriant in the sensual sun
And tossed by wind's intricacies,
And finds repose is more than grief
When failing light and falling leaf
Denote that winter has begun.

AT THE WINDOW

Then more-than-morning quiet
The pretty lawn extended;
And rooted trees stood tall
On westward shadows pointing.

Answering no will, my hand
Dropped from the window catch,
My throat was undecided
Whether to sob or sing.

Why trees were not, nor morning,
No flash of mind revealed,
But throat and hands had greeted
A memory more clear than sight.

WINTER SPECULATION

We have travelled to a new country,
A region of hills
Where the sky is a frosted glass
Splintered with branches.
Winter piles up against the window ledges;
In our hearts the drifts deepen.
We are in a new country
And estranged.

Were you to die here,
Being delicate –
Were you to die after a season
And winter to surrender the hilltops finally,
Would not the whiteness melt from our hearts
And the river break
And I be left
Alone in the sunlight in a new country?

Here they tell me
Winter is long
Almost to forgetting spring.

THOUGHTS AND MEMORIES

Do others waking in the morning hear
Dog bark or cuckoo call
And suddenly not know for certain whether
Dog or bird was there at all?
Perhaps a poacher or a country boy
Is never taken unawares
But active with his snares
Is not so caught up in the past as I.

Do you too wonder if the finest thing
A promising flower can do
Is but to imitate with all its art
All other flowers that ever grew?
You looking from your window see the spring
Each year perform its leisurely
Long act of memory,
All nature gone into remembering.

Do you too lying sleepless think of things
That you have said or done,
Communicate with ghosts and fantasies
As if you feared to be alone?
You start to fall asleep, and one by one
Thoughts and memories go their ways;
You sleep and no ghost stays –
And oh, the horror if you waken them!

from
The Imprisoned Sea
(1949)

THE DANCERS

Too late he saw the watcher in the shade
Signal from the laurels beside the lawn,
The circle close and the loved figure vanish
In a maze of pointed feet, a flash of hair.
He heard the leaves of the sycamore complain.

Now to the garden the lapsed years recall
No cloaked betrayer and no mythical dancers
Who steal by moonlight in the month of August.
Instead, upon the lawn together pace
A child's ghost and a man of ageing heart.

THE CONSPIRATORS 1940

'Talk of the green time and birds on branches'
Said the ragged robin to the lords and ladies.
'Read him the tale of love ever after,'
The blackbird whistled in the summer wind.

'Your kind attention, your smooth enticements
Are vain distractions,' the listener said.
'Your knee-high grasses, your cavernous hedgerows,
Are secret as treason but they cannot hide

The man in blue lying deep in the ditch,
His eyes gaping, his limbs askew,
And out of his nonchalant mouth a trickle
Red and crooked as the rivers of Hell.'

BESTIARY

Happy the quick-eyed lizard that pursues
   Its creviced zigzag race
Amid the epic ruins of a temple
   Leaving no trace.

Happy the weasel in the moonlit churchyard
   Twisting a vibrant thread
Of narrow life between the mounds that hide
   The important dead.

Close to the complex fabric of their world
   The small beasts live who shun
The spaces where the huge ones bellow, fight,
   And snore in the sun.

How admirable the modest and the frugal,
   The small, the neat, the furtive.
How troublesome the mammoths of the world,
   Gross and assertive.

Happy should we live in the interstices
   Of a declining age,
Even while the impudent masters of decision
   Trample and rage.

MISGIVINGS

Ask me no question now or any night,
Ask no question, dearest, and forgive,
If now and then I stop to hark
As the wind fidgets in the dark
Outside the window – if I have no ear
For you, but seem to hear
Something as an old fox gone to ground
Might hear a certain half-forgotten sound
Or stiffen at a scent which crept
About him as he slept.

Uneasiness like this can instantly
Turn all into a dream –
Yes, and make your eyes seem
Violets in woods irrevocably lost.

GREENHALLOWS

All the omens were good, the air smelt of success.
The sun soared over the defeated mist.
I had broken no shoelace, shaved without mishap.
My toga swung handsomely.
The train bounded between the silver roofs.
A girl in muslin with a skipping-rope
Waved from a courtyard. The wires saluted me.
'Greenhallows' – pretty name. Reading between
The careful lines in the personal column
I visualised a sort of chauffeur-secretary
Reliable and relied on as I moved
Expertly among the week-end guests,
Good birth my passport, travel my education.
I thought of the starry-eyed, the exiles,
The handkerchiefs along the quay –
And now for me no more
The accordion in the sailors' café,
The olive-islands grey with anguish, blurred.
I smoothed my clothes
And straightened my chaplet of acanthus.

Lawn-green are the halls in that superb mansion,
Sea-green the carpet sweeping up the stair
To where you hear in fancy
From nile-green bathrooms siren voices sing.
Somewhere amidst porcelain and laughter
You imagine the guests
Heavy-lipped, high-cheeked, beautiful,
Listening with their eyes.

To those on the sun-roof
Boys with indifferent classic brows carry soft drinks.
Out in the garden languid waters play,
In the house music from hidden strings.
Remote dynamos make power and light.
Birds of foreign plumage, coppery, dark,
Circle about the electric chandeliers.

I was left alone, wondering
Whether it was really morning or evening.
Whether the servants had lied about the time.
How it was the murals were of my design
And why the signatures in the visitors' book –
Senators', athletes', film stars' (even some
Of yours, my friends) – were all in my own writing!
As I entered, why had I felt distinctly
As if someone had just replaced
The ornaments by others of my choice?
Then what was it they had said in the village
About 'attempts' and 'interference'? Was that the reason
For the debris imperfectly concealed
Under a tarpaulin by the garage?
Why the fire in August? Why
The unmistakable odour of disinfectant?

A door clicks. Discreet feet
Ripple the sea-green floor.
'Mr Presumption? My name is Wheels.
Her ladyship will be down directly. In the meantime –
As I hand over my reference from the priest
I see it is marked with fingerprints of sweat.

My ears hum. A sound of sawing, then
An angel-voice, thin-souled like the wind
Threading a colonnade of icicles –
Mine! a record made at choir-school years ago
'I'm not quite well – I ought to catch the next train back.'
'Train? But there's no station – '
Lies! 'We had it moved
On account of the noise.' Falsehood! deceit!
The green walls swim apart, the floor rocks,
All revolves. Blackness ... and then
A cool hand, something to drink, white and bitter.
My eyes open and see
The stone smile of a queen
The bust of Minerva on a public building
The Lady of Greenhallows.
My friends, pity me. You have been there
You have all been to Greenhallows in your time.
Yes, though you tore your diaries and re-tore them
And watched the fragments shrivel, you remember.
I need not tell you how I ran,
My chaplet fallen, my toga disarrayed.
I noticed the door was marked 'Out Patients'
And a man in a white coat raged and flapped.
The green vistas that deluded, you have seen them
And heard the mocking music that pursued me.
We shall keep, my friends, among us
This unshared secret, the shame and the elation,
One day shall we make, perhaps, together,
A journey without omens and mistrust the weather?

AEONS HENCE

When, aeons hence, they rediscover
The unregarded island I inhabit,
Will they not marvel
How life upon so bare a soil withstood
This testy climate and abrasive sea?

And when by excavation
My relics are exposed, my habits known,
How, perching on a ledge out of the wind,
I scraped a living, will they not admit
They've lost the secret of some things I did,
As making good pots from this gritty clay
And music from a certain kind of shells?

MUSIC IN THE WOOD

Music there would be of horns far off.
Sombre and dolorous through the wood it came
To where we faltered in the darkening track.

The trees are taller now. Should I return,
That seminal music – would it still he heard,
Those notes again congeal my errant blood,
A cruel shiver at the spine recall
The wind lamenting in the perjured valley?
With what unclouded mind the man might then
Witness the marvel that perturbed the child.

FOR YEARS WE TRACED

For years we traced the river back,
A month of swamps for two of scree.
The beasts all died, the boys turned back.
For years we had not said
'Above the next fall the promised view
The green, rewarding view.'
What we had seen no one said.

One struck the sun-cursed rock,
Recited fearing for his mind
Time and again the shepherd's dirge,
Less for the death he had in mind
Than for the Shakespeare phrase.

One kept, he says, before his eyes
A picture by a Spanish master,
A peasant's brooding eyes
And tilted lustrous wine.
I saw the columned temple in the haze
As its designer saw it first
Immaculate, finished in the sunset haze.

Bound in our spirit's isolation
These we felt we could appraise.
Bound by the thwarted enterprise
We thought we knew the worth of praise.
These, not the legendary land,
The impossible land towards the source,
Were what our vision played on,
And had been for years.

TWO MINDS

Stone-eyed, with a sculpture-lion look,
The old man in his garden stares
From centuries of correctitude.
His fine nostrils slightly note
The October bonfires of his neighbours;
His brow disdains
The charred fragments on his border.
I, hovering between the gravel and the turf,
Between talk and musing, glance
Now at my host and now at where
The tall flowers violet and blue
Grouped in perennial sisterhood
Surpass a seedsman's fantasy.

Seeing the many roofs of many neighbours
The half-made gardens of the more to come
And the old man aloof,
Sedate lineage scarce affronted,
I hover between two minds rejecting both:
The feeling of 'all this has been before,
It all happened to me long ago' –
Only a re-enacting
Could be so graphic, so composed –
The doubt that none the less
What is new is ineffectual
Since tenure of history
So long enjoyed not even death disputes.

THOUGHTS INDOORS

Never ask questions walking on a lawn.
The unanswered ones still bring the garden ghosts
    Too numerous already
To bandy them among the leaves till dawn.
    Let perfumes vain and sweet
    Wander there
  But in such presence-ridden air
Question no more for idlers to repeat.

Never ask questions off the shore of sleep.
The nodding masts would bear you into port.
    Voyaging-time is over.
Let speculations till the morning keep.
    Away from this smooth shore
    Are doubtful seas.
  Think if you will of certainties,
But better now to sleep and think no more.

Ask questions at your hearth, the place of answers.
Think where thoughts end in thought, not ghosts or sleep,
    Where you alone are hearer
And round your books the moths are heedless dancers.
    Then moths at last expel
    To ghosts and flowers
  And give to sleep the sleepy hours
When your four walls have nothing more to tell.

A MATTER OF DISCIPLINE

Paunch foremost, shambling, dilatory,
The school porter came to the school play.
Although we call him sergeant-major
Nothing of him now is military
Except perhaps his waxed moustaches.
But when he saw those mimic soldiers,
The slovenly parade-ground antics,
And heard the callow actors mock
The old commands, who knows what stirred
Of an obscure allegiance hidden
In his slack nerves, to protest bidden?
Perhaps an instant's brief suspension
Of many years' passivity
His unused muscles mobilised
To stand correctly to attention.

from
The Password
(1952)

THE TREE OF LIFE

I shared my garden with the tree of life,
   In whose bewildering and populous maze
Delicious birds conspired incessantly
   To steal and squander all my earnest days.

And in my room at night and in my ears
   The cunning voices of the leaves would creep.
Riddling predictions, twilight menaces
   Twitched the uneasy curtains of my sleep.

I strove one night beneath a murderer's moon
   With sharpest stroke and self-destructive rage
To fell the monster or at least some boughs
   For it was proud and obdurate with age.

And when it groaned at my demented blows
   And shuddered fearfully from bole to bud,
I saw with cry of horror on my breath
   The ground below was overrun with blood.

I share my garden with the deathless tree.
   My days and nights those voices still entrap.
What was the image by the storm-tossed moon?
   The tree of life has blood instead of sap.

A VIOLIN CONCERTO

Now is the focus of all hopes:
    She poises on the topmost stair.
And many-candled, many-tongued
    Anticipation buoys her there.

Her beauty is her own spotlight:
    As she descends, the talking dies;
And crystal lustres shine no more
    Than tears that start in ladies' eyes.

Her face is lit with holy joy,
    Her body moves in ice and flame;
He who looks into her eyes
    Can understand the Trojan shame.

The hubbub of the strings subsides;
    And now the final drums proclaim
The solo violin which sings
    The union of ice and flame.

Courageous tunes that like a girl
    Can the listening crowd compel –
Perfection alone like this divides
    The human soul from death and hell.

Wolfgang Mozart's violin
    Leads me to the living stream;
There if I drink, the black abyss
    Is no more than a troubling dream.

HAD I PASSION TO MATCH MY SKILL

Had I passion to match my skill,
I would not hear the worm complain,
The worm that frets and mumbles still
In the corridors of my brain.

The flames that burn inside my heart,
On what fuel do they feed?
I the mystery would impart,
Had I skill to match my need.

Had I passion and skill
To match my daring will,
I would rise and seek
The stony path that scales the virgin peak.

Between my hands I hold my brain,
Between my ribs I nurse a fire;
Beyond my utmost step remain
The summits where the goats aspire.

Inside my brain the worm revolves,
The heart consumes inside my breast;
And so I sit, and nothing solves
The puzzles that are not expressed.

LEAVING TOWN

It was impossible to leave the town.
Bumping across a maze of obsolete rails
Three times we reached the gasworks and reversed.
We could not get away from the canal;
Dead cats, dead hopes, in those grey deeps immersed,
Over our efforts breathed a spectral prayer.
The cattle-market and the gospel-hall
Returned like fictions of our own despair,
And like Hesperides the suburbs seemed,
Shining far off towards the guiltless fields.
We finished in a little cul-de-sac
Where on the pavement sat a ragged girl
Mourning beside a jug-and-bottle entrance.
Once more we turned the car and started back.

IN THE TRAIN

She is the passenger with restless eyes
Who twists the ticket in her black-gloved fingers.
None knows what calculation, what surmise
Disturb her as the train jerks on or lingers.
Above the eyes her brow is smooth and yellow.
'I grant,' her silence says, 'that all I planned
Has been like something graven in the sand,
But tell me how *your* schemes work out, my fellow.'

IN THE CLUBHOUSE

In the clubhouse are exchanged banalities,
    Also commercial privileges. A lavish odour
Circles the heads of houses when they scheme;
    And the river of time flows down like brandy-and-soda.

The cleverest heads will be crowned with genuine gold,
    Crowns of gold for the strongest. No one supposes
That she behind the bar is a queen incognita
    And will reward the loser with a crown of wild roses.

Not on a white liner she came, first class,
    From Jamaica, Manila, Kenya or the west –
No, but from blue Sicilian fields with her head full
    Of doves in the silver trees telling of rest.

THE PRISONERS

Somehow we never escaped
   Into the sunlight,
Though the gates were always unbarred
   And the warders tight.
For the sketches on the walls
   Were to our liking,
And squeaks from the torture-cell
   Most satisfying.

A FIRE I LIT

A fire I lit to warm my hands
   Blazed out and leapt upon the floor.
It burnt to ashes my tall house
   And left me colder than before.

THE LITTLE BROTHER

God! how they plagued his life, the three damned sisters,
Throwing stones at him out of the cherry trees,
Pulling his hair, smudging his exercises,
Whispering. How passionately he sees
His spilt minnows flounder in the grass.

There will be sisters subtler far than these,
Baleful and dark, with slender, cared-for hands,
Who will not smirk and babble in the trees,
But feed him with sweet words and provocations,
And in his sleep practise their sorceries,
Appearing in the form of ragged clouds
And at the corners of malignant seas.

As with his wounded life he goes alone
To the world's end, where even tears freeze,
He will in bitter memory and remorse
Hear the lost sisters innocently tease.

OLD CRABBED MEN

This old crabbed man, with his wrinkled, fusty clothes
And his offensive smell – who would suppose
That in his day he invented a new rose
Exciting still the fastidious eye and nose?

That old crabbed man, sloven of speech and dress,
Was once known among women – who would now
    guess? –
As a lover of the most perfect address,
Reducing the stubbornest beauty to nakedness.

This old crabbed man, pattering and absurd,
With a falsetto voice – which of you has heard
How in his youth he mastered the lyric word?
His unflawed verse spoke like a March bird.

FRAGMENTS OF A LANDSCAPE

The uninhabitable moon
Rejects her lifelong worshippers
Who long since knelt upon the shore
Raising their arms for pity and relief
Until they flaked to skeletons.

We walked together on the strand
Eye in eye and hand in hand.
You could not see my mouth was full of sand,
Like a blind statue that could no more stand.
You could not hear the waves that beat
Tumultuous in the chambers of my heart,
Forcing their walls apart,
Till I had no desire except to be
One with the kneeling bones
Among the seabirds and the seaworn stones.

VULTURE ABSENCE

Now dies the world beneath the smothering cloud.
The vulture absence waits upon us two.
We question from what loveless hell he flew.

Because, dear love, at parting we are proud
To think you live in me and I in you,
Now dies the world beneath the smothering cloud;
The vulture absence waits upon us two.

So in my arms your body cries aloud;
Flesh upon bone since we together grew,
The hours torment, the ragged wings pursue.
Now dies the world beneath the smothering cloud.
The vulture absence waits upon us two.
We question from what loveless hell he flew.

A SONNET IN WINTER

Imagine, north of everywhere, a chain
Of stark untrodden mountains to embrace
The whole world's cold and every hurricane,
So that there never was a stormier place.
Imagine then that every cold wind lay
As in a prison there for ever curled:
'O hills of charity,' all men would say,
'Thus to keep angry winter from the world.'
They would be wrong. Mountains of desert stone
For loneliness, not charity, their arms
Would fold about the winter's rudest blast.
Both loneliness and mountains I have known;
And I would keep you so, imprisoned fast,
Although I held against my heart all storms.

NOVELS I HAVE NEVER WRITTEN

From novels I have never written
The ghosts have long departed,
Leaving tenantless the Sussex country houses
And the palazzo steps brown with moss.
Only the foundations remain
On which were to have risen
The towers and cloisters of the fatal school.
In the unfinished rooms
The conversations have shivered into silence.
The moving incidents,
The revealing situations,
The moments of profound psychological insight –
All are lost, unwanted,
Like garden furniture rusting in a summer-house.
All the ghosts have departed, unaccounted for,
Some perhaps for South America,
Others to get what employment they can
As car-park attendants and waiters in seaside hotels,
Or they have simply died.

Only the disconsolate hero survives,
Sitting on an upturned packing-case in an empty house,
With the electricity and the telephone cut off,
Nothing to eat, no money, and nowhere to go.
Too round a character to disappear quietly,
Too big a man to be pensioned off or eased into a sinecure.
Presently, perhaps, he will reappear in Oxford
As one of those dusty, forgotten dons whom I have heard
Talking to themselves in the High,

Or a faded roué living on the Côte d'Azur
On the savings of a discarded opera-singer –
Someone who can sustain the pretence
Of having been influential in former days,
The intimate of writers, friends of diplomats ...

THE INFERNAL MACHINE

I am delicate-winged like a butterfly
As I shimmer down to rest on the sands
Or the Downs near Beachy Head.
I am tempting as a packet of chocolate,
Nougat, fudge or marshmallow
All shiny with cellophane.
I smile beneficently like a spectacled teacher.

But don't come near me, children – I am dangerous.
If you touch me, I go off,
And your trustful enquiring eyes,
Your expectant fingers and excited heart
Will all be blown to smithereens
And you will be none the wiser.

THE STONE GENTLEMAN

Let us move the stone gentleman to the toadstool wood:
Too long has he disapproved in our market-place.
Within the manifold stone creases of his frock-coat
    Let the woodlouse harbour and thrive.

Let the hamadryads wreath him with bryony,
The scrolled fern-fronds greenly fantasticate,
And sappy etiolations cluster damply
    About the paternal knee.

Them the abrupt, blank eyes will not offend.
The civic brow and raised, suppressive hand
Unchallenged and without affront shall manage
    The republic of tall spiders.

COUNSEL TO BOYS

At Holy Trinity beside the quay
   The grey one touched my arm and pointed up.
'Some poor soul going home,' she said to me.

And in her eyes I saw the mourners pass
   And with her parchment ears I heard the chant
Raised for the dead bound in with lacquered brass.

A sea-wind like the passage of a soul
   Fluttered her torn remains and she was gone.
To all alike comes at the end such dole.

Therefore, rash youngster on the bridge at play
   Near where the old men lean and fish for nothing,
Better than do as they do, I would say,

Since all are paid their funerary verses,
   Better it is to study to grow rich
And own at last a fleet of plated hearses.

How better to serve the poor ones of your city
   Than carry them in decent splendour home,
And thus on all grey ragged souls take pity?

'A LETTER TO POSTERITY'
suggested by a radio series under that title

This I would say. I see you perfectly
In your unfashionable favourite chair,
With knees drawn up and cheek on fist, your page
Shadowed by indeterminate brown hair.

You read of us perhaps, or think of him,
The unmitigable man who steals your mind;
I hear you sigh, and see you smile, and wonder
What comedy in us or him you find.

We have philosophers, and so have you.
'Our age' they say, not knowing what they mean;
But I can tell you, dear, what our age is,
What yours is too, and others all have been.

Cities and ships we purpose for your ease,
To see you grateful, smiling in your chair;
If we forget, or fail, or you turn peevish,
We break and burn in fury of despair.

Ask that dark man who blunders through your thoughts
Why from the precipice he brings you flowers;
Smile on him if you can: only your smile
Can make his age a better age than ours.

POET OF BIRDS
JCR

Lost bird, dead bird, dove, peacock, nightingale –
They fly and cry their way through all your page.
If it is liberty they symbolise,
How were you prisoner then, and in what cage?

from

The Talking Skull

(1958)

TO NORMAN CAMERON 1905-1953

I asked the river-god a song
With which to mourn your fallen head.
No answer: but a low wind crept
About the stones of his dry bed.

The fingers of insomnia
Turning the pages of self-hate
Are like the incurious wind that stirred
The papery reeds on that estate.

In other days I knew the god
Who flashed and chuckled in the sun.
Where has he taken now his moods
Of shadow and his sense of fun?

The requiem I might have had
From him you would have understood:
Just as you also understood
How hard a thing it is, though good,

To hold your tongue and wait your time
When there is nothing to be said.
I know it now: I knew you both
But he is gone, and you are dead.

Even the wind has died; no sound
In this dull air is born to live;
So I my desperate silences
To you my friend and poet give.

THIS MOOD OF MURDER

Say who brought murder to the quiet street,
To read his guilt in their white eyes
And in the acceleration of their feet:
Say who brought murder to the quiet street
And I will say my name.
     You should look pale
To hear the bells' resentful beat
Tolling, tolling his retreat.
You should look pale to understand his tale
In their white eyes and ticking feet.
Say who brought murder to the quiet street
And I will say my name.
     But should you pale
To meet his accomplice in your looking-glass,
Then go to bed alone with one who spread
This mood of murder in a quiet street.

'AND SO THEY CAME TO LIVE AT DAFFODIL WATER'

'And so they came to live at Daffodil Water.'
Such were the words that fell as by dictation
Into the cloud of my preoccupation,
And one by one they fluttered down like leaves,
Touching me with their strange illumination –
Like leaves the girls would catch at Butler's Cross
To bring themselves good luck, each leaf a year.

'And so they came to live at Daffodil Water.'
A grey-green light of depths that do not stir
Beneath the unfledged ash-bough's contemplation
Touches me now as I transcribe the words.
Such were the depths perhaps where Hylas drowned,
Such were the wreaths his temptresses would wear.
But who are *they* who came to shelter there
And live obscurely by that leaf-light crowned,
Patiently mending their storm-shattered minds?

Who came to live in grace at Daffodil Water,
And why they sheltered there and from what storm,
Neither the voice that speaks through my abstraction
Nor my own fantasy serves to inform.

ON A POET

E.B. 1896-1973

Having no Celtic bombast in his blood,
Nor dipsomaniac rage, nor very much
To give his time of what his time expected,
He saw his Muse, slight thing, by most neglected.

She was no exhibitionist, and he,
With only the Queen or Elfland's gift to Thomas,
Could not afford to school her in the taste
For stolen gauds and ornaments of paste.

When he is dead and his best phrases stored
With Clare's and Hardy's in the book of gold,
She with her unpresuming Saxon grace
In the Queen's retinue will take her place.

THE TALK

They talked of Dr Graham and the Church,
And William Moss the Labour candidate.
I thought how once I would have thought of you,
Of Dido's tears and of the shears of fate.

I would have thought of you and how you spoke
Of Picquette in her dress of cobweb-grey,
And of the six fauns' eyes between the saplings –
The lost girls, and the bad man in the play.

But when I thought of what I should recall,
Feeling, regret, and memory I had none.
Treason is absolute; it need not be
Treason to anything or anyone.

So, with a sense of treason overhead
Clouding my mind, I followed the debate.
We talked of Dr Graham and the Church.
We talked of Moss the Labour candidate.

AN ACADEMIC

How sad, they think, to see him homing nightly
In converse with himself across the quad,
Down by the river and the railway arch
To his gaunt villa and his squabbling brood,
His wife anchored beside a hill of mending.
Such banal evenings – how they pity him.

By day his food is Plato, Machiavelli,
'Thought is a flower, gentlemen,' he says –
Tracing the thought in air until it grows
Like frost-flowers on the windows of the mind –
'Thought is a flower that has its roots in dung.'
What irony, they think, that one so nourished,
Perfect in all the classic commonwealths,
Himself so signally should lack the arts
To shine and burgeon in the College councils,
A worn-out battery, a nobody, a windbag.
'And yet,' they sigh, 'what has the old boy got,
That every time he talks he fills the hall?'

HOMAGE TO THE MOTH

At half-past two a moth flew in
To look for something in my room.
I had abandoned long before
The revelations of the night.
Was it a memory she sought
Or an escape? or did she come
Simply to substantiate
Some man-invented myth of moths
Which calls them souls of god or queen?
Well then, suppose this dowdy soul
To be my own especial queen
Who now had come to spy on me.
Were there not proofs of my devotion
(Though she had broken faith with me) –
Papers awry on my desk,
Eleven cancelled lines of verse?
But should this proof not satisfy,
Let her reflect that since a queen
Might roam in likeness of a moth
A poem too might be transformed.
Then some nocturnal, crazy sound,
Cock-crow, cat-call or hoot of owl,
Might be my homage to the moth.

from
The Questioning Tiger
(1964)

EVOLUTION OF A PAINTER

Beneath a pastoral sky, spotted by shadows,
Only by your young, talented eye regarded,
The two farm horses stood, unkempt and useful.
Your heart approved as your deft brush recorded.
One notes the skill; surprised, one notes the love,
And pensive, calm content the scene afforded.

For that was forty years ago, since when
The stoical farm beast has been abolished.
Not so your art, though now the patrons call
For something more expensive and embellished.
Proudly your valuable racers prance
Over the emerald turf, well combed and polished.

We need not twist our mouths with scorn to see
A pretty talent gone corrupt and hard.
Better than you have sold out for champagne.
Enough to know there is, where few regard,
The evidence of your compassion once,
In that ill-lit provincial gallery stored.

IMPORTANT INSECTS

Important insects clamber to the top
Of stalks; look round with uninquiring eyes
And find the world incomprehensible;
Then totter back to earth and circumscribe
Irregular territories pointlessly.
Some insects narcissistically assume
Patterns of spots or stripes or burnished sheen
For purposes of sex or camouflage,
Some tweet or rasp, though most are without speech
Except a low, subliminal, mindless chatter.
Take heart: those scientists are wrong who find
Elements of the human in their systems,
Despite their busy, devious trafficking
Important insects simply do not matter.

DE FESCH

For you I search my reference books in vain,
Willem of the impossible name De Fesch.
Vienna was it, Venice, or Amsterdam
Whose plain citizens knew you in the flesh?

Midnight has fallen; the wind unpacified
Moves in the outer darkness while I think
Of that odd sound: not grand, like Palestrina,
Nor quaint, like Dittersdorf or Humperdinck.

Willem de Fesch would seem to be a sound
Not shaped predestinately for high fame;
Nevertheless to-night it pleases me
To celebrate your spirit with your name.

By way of certain pieces for two 'cellos
That spirit earlier breathed upon the air.
Even in an age renowned for melody
Your phrase was of a quality so rare
It spoke out of no time to any time
When a dry heart might wither from despair.

A STOICAL ROBIN

'A stoical robin solid in the drift' –
I coined the line some seven years ago.
The poem was a failure, but those words
Return to memorise a famous snow.

In fact he wasn't dead. We took him in,
And put him down beside the fire to thaw.
He neither ate our crumbs nor drank our water
But, once revived, true to some primal law,

Took wing and vanished through the open window.
It seemed he'd not accept life as a gift
From those who live in houses, but would rather
Hazard for liberty the frozen drift.

Well, I might follow this excogitation
Into some parable of the human plight.
Instead I conjure from my inner view
A bird whose wings were never spread for flight,

A captive goldfinch chained against a wall.
Was it pity, anger, or despair
Or simply with a painter's eye for colour
The Dutchman, Carl Fabritius, put him there?

The brilliant plumes are folded, the head firm:
Indifferent or contemptuous, the eyes brood.
A passionless fidelity to nature
Covers the painter's real attitude.

So I may take the chained bird, if I choose,
As emblematic of the mind of man;
And I salute the all-but-unknown artist,
Whether or not this was his conscious plan.

My robin's nothing, but your goldfinch lives,
Becomes an artefact by your success.
Yours lives in freedom, one might say, while mine
Remains imprisoned in my feebleness.

DISCHARGED FROM HOSPITAL

He stands upon the steps and fronts the morning.
The porter has called a taxi, and behind him
The infirmary doors have swung and come to rest.
Physician, surgeon, and anaesthetist
Have exercised their skill and he is cured.
The rabelaisian sister with the bedpan,
The vigorous masseuse, the sensual nurse
Who washes him modestly beneath a blanket,
The dawn chorus of cleaners, the almoner,
The visiting clergyman – all proceed without him.
He is alone beyond all need of them,
And the saved man goes home, to die of health.

NO TEARS FOR MISS MACASSAR

No tears for Miss Macassar, dispossessed
Three times by an inflexible landlord
Of that small tenement in which she housed
Her ominous, gaunt person and the hoard
Of keepsakes, water-colours, ferns and china.
She and her framed, clerical relations
Now to fresh scenes remove and to new neighbours.
She, stoical connoisseur of all privations,
Treasures her grievances like vintage wine.
So tears for Miss Macassar would be wrong:
She is no miser and too well she knows
Good wine is better shared than kept too long.

DEMIGODS

We demigods can't be too careful, see.
Stricter proprieties hedge us. One slip-up
Can get us a bad name both in heaven and earth.
One of us lies or cheats and some god says
Well, he's half-human – what can you expect?
Another whores or drinks himself to death
And all men vilify his godly vices.
It's hard. But with the gods, how different!

All that they do enhances their prestige,
Or is officially overlooked; or else
Is twisted to adorn the personal legends
They've nothing else to do but manufacture.

Incest or sodomy, it's all the same,
A god must have some respite from his cares.
And erring humans claim divine protection;
But demigods have got to mind their step.

GENERATION OF A CRITIC

The eager eye that went with you to school
Reported birds' eggs in the thicket;
The heart your mother and your father split
Was healed by girls and village cricket.

The euphuistic tongue and pen you practised
To gain no other recognition
Than that boon friend's you walked or drank beside.
Then Satan told you of ambition.

He whispered fame, wealth, power – and all that;
He promised honorary degrees;
He told you no one ever made a name
By cutting other names in trees.

So now the eager eye that went to school
With jealousy has gone a-squint;
The tongue is shrill, the ink turned poison,
Getting and keeping you in print.

BRUGES

And here, in the tiny city of the unloved,
Every third shop-window is a confectioner's,
In which daily on their walk from work
The mundane inhabitants eat heaven with their eyes.
That other heaven to which their faith consigns them
Is meanwhile populated only by sugar-angels
And the notes of bells
Breaking quarter-hourly from sky-high stone imprisonment
Like birds on scattered crumbs.
So lives the generation of the hungry
In a city piled with sweetmeats.

THE TIGER

They have sat in their wide window and approved
Irregularities of the autumn sky
Between the coasts of the sycamore and yew.
They have banished the questioning tiger from their land
Who might have resurrected the old fear
Springing like joy in the striped glades of childhood.
They have long known that the pursuing beasts
That strike at them on waking are themselves,
Have ceased to love the tiger for his hate.

PLANNING PERMISSION

He looked at me without surprise or pleasure
But with a bored, habitual compassion.
'They sent me here,' I said. 'I want to build.'
'Naturally,' he said. 'We'll see what we can do.'
Along the hopeless counter twenty others
Were seeing what they could do.
                       'You'll need these forms.'
Application for permission for an erection
For occupation as residential accommodation
And/or private domestic habitation.
'In triplicate of course. Return when filled
To the assistant sub-divisional officer.'
I took the papers. Tears of gratitude
Misted my sight; but he was gone already
Into the wastes beneath his sandy hair.

I took the papers back.
Alone in his little room
The assistant sub-divisional sent for me.
He looked at me without surprise or pleasure
But with compassionate unrecognition.
'Permission for an erection. Quite so. We'll write.'
'Oh thank you, sir,' I started. 'Do you think ...?'
But underneath the sandy hair the eyes were blank.
After eleven months the answer came.
'Rejection of permission for an erection.
Any appeal to be directed within three years
To the sub-divisional officer for attention.'

Two years and more went by before I gained
The sub-divisional officer's section. With relief
I saw that he at least had had his due reward.
Between the flat ears under the greying hair
No sign of recognition stirred.
                              'Ah yes.
Objection to rejection of application for erection.'
With the old bored compassion in his voice,
'We'll do,' he promised, 'what we can to help.'
'Oh sir,' I sobbed. He interrupted me.
'I'll pass on your objection to the divisional officer.
It may take time.'
                    Re-charged with hope I went.

I died; and here I falter by the gate
Drained of desire and too ashamed to face
The sorrowing figure on the throne of grace.

POOR WOMAN

She backed him for a win
In the Immortality Stakes.
Here, she thought, is someone
Who amounts to something
Or something which amounts
To someone.
For fifty mortal years
She has endured his vanity,
Duplicity, boorishness, insensitivity –
And what is her reward?
Tired, harassed and grey,
As the mourners go, she says:
To hell with immortality. Thank God that's over.
Her own immortal lot she has endured daily
For fifty years, is now
Heartily sick of it.

IMPROVISATIONS

1
Plastic

This popular wreath, the plastic model,
   Which only the vulgar-hearted crave,
Will last when every swollen noddle
   That wears it will be in the grave.
Yet who'd preserve a thing so cheap,
   So dearly bought at any cost?
Its place is on the rubbish heap:
   True fame is neither sought nor lost.

2
Be Certain, Mr A—Z

Be Certain, Mr A to Z,
   That when the vulture drops its dirt
Upon your undistinguished head
   It is not chance but your desert.

3
To Be is Love

To be, and not to think, is love:
So while I love you, love, I am,
Not less because I prize the light
More than the heat of this live flame.
Irrational love is like the bird

That serenades the setting sun
And sings upon the orchard top
Despite the farmer and his gun.

4
Precept

Dwell in some decent corner of your being,
Where plates are orderly set and talk is quiet,
Not in its devious crooked corridors
Nor in its halls of riot.

5
Things to Come

The shadow of a fat man in the moonlight
    Precedes me on the road down which I go;
And should I turn and run, he would pursue me:
    This is the man whom I must get to know.

INDIRECT SPEECH

Schoolmasters regularly fulminate
Against the horrors of official jargon;
And yet if these reformers had their way
I'm not so sure we'd get a better bargain.

Although admittedly periphrasis
Imparts an air of unreality,
Under the circumstances now obtaining
It might be better to let evil be.

To-day I had a buff, official notice
Couched in the smoothest, most obsequious terms;
But what it meant was: 'We can break you, Reeves;
You'd better pay up quick, you worm of worms!'

GOAT AND COMPASSES

By etymologies of public houses
Many are tempted to rash speculation.
This 'Goat and Compasses', where now we tend,
Must surely have a likelier derivation
Than 'God encompasseth us' – such irony
Could any mind unprejudiced admit?
Step to the bar and order what you will,
And in our private angle as we sit
These compasses can signify the force
That holds our thoughts within the civil order;
The goat obscenely leads them in a dance
Up to the outlaw country on the border.
The anarchic goat and rational compasses,
These are the warring standards that divide:
But here in conference in our private angle
Under this sign our thoughts are pacified.

THE SOLVERS

Invalids and other hotel residents
Unpuzzle themselves with patience-cards and jigsaws.
Crosswords engage saloon passengers at sea.
Philosophers invent puzzles with answers.
Each knows that what he is trying *can* be done.
Not all enjoy such comfort of assurance.
I, watching the backs of houses and of books,
Work away at my mind, fitting the pieces,
Pairing the cards, rejecting words.
So sitting, I become suddenly conscious
Of playing patience with crooked pieces,
While solving an incomplete jigsaw with words
In the precise non-language of a dream.
Some of the pieces fit, some of the cards match,
Only some of the pieces and the cards are lost.
I have tried to play it according to the rules,
Only the rules they sent are in Chinese.
Is it too late, I ask, to start again?
Or will extinction, when it comes, surprise me
Sorting the pieces, working out the clues?

GRAND OPERA

The lovers have poisoned themselves and died singing,
And the crushed peasant father howls in vain.
For his duplicity, lubricity and greed
The unspeakable base count is horribly slain.

After the music, after the applause,
The lights go up, the final curtain drops.
The clerks troop from the house, and some are thinking:
Why is life different when the singing stops?

All that hysteria and those histrionics,
All those coincidences were absurd.
But if there no relevance to life,
Why were they moved to shudder and applaud?

Though they outlived that passion, it was theirs,
As was the jealousy, the sense of wrong
When some proud jack-in-office trampled them;
Only it did not goad them into song.

The accidents, the gross misunderstandings,
Paternal sorrow, amorous frustration
Have they not suffered? Was the melodrama
An altogether baseless imitation?

from
Subsong
(1969)

ALL DAYS BUT ONE

All days but one shall see us wake to make
Our last confession:
Bird notes at dawn revive the night's obsession.

In this dark light I need not see to be
My own confessor:
Crime still is crime, the greater and the lesser.

There is no calculus we know can show,
No sum can prove,
Love that is three parts guilt is one part love.

We conjure from some inner place the face,
Perhaps the voice
On which we fix what we must call our choice.

Not these console us, but some word we heard
Or thought we heard
When doubts awake us with the waking bird.

The saving word of love we thought we caught
Might have redeemed,
Could we be certain it was said, not dreamed.

But when the love we would have built on guilt
Is mere illusion,
Bird notes at dawn repeat the night's confusion.

THIS CORRUPT MUSIC

This corrupt music of the violin –
Its consolations fail the inveterate ear,
Satiate with formal, timeless eloquence.
He groans to be relieved from absolute beauty
By the warm impact of ephemeral life.
The music extracts from naked flesh,
Unheard and unrecorded, needs no score.

Only the fully lived can fully die.
What the inveterate ear supposes lived
Fell short of life. The unconsoling phrase
Speaks what it never knew, corrupt in beauty;
What never lived lives now in its corruption.
Death is the silent tune flesh plays on flesh.

SONG (THE SLEEP I LOST)

The sleep I lost for you last night
I might have found at break of day
Had not the lapidary birds
These waking words conspired to say:

The only hell is guilt unshared;
A silence shared need not be broken.
The worst of love is not to speak;
The best of love is never spoken.

METAMORPHOSIS

You found, by small hours of your running feet,
The coastal waters sliding, insect wings,
And voices multifarious amid leaves,
Not knowing then
The territories of your big desire
By time's enormity would turn
To little wicked areas of flesh;
And now when feet are slow,
Dawn birds mere carrion
The alps and thickets of the needed body
Are inaccessible as voices speaking
Across the rise and fall of classic fountains.
What would the senses give, you ask, for such
An instant context for their morning play,
A warm and actual territory in flesh?

THE MEETING

There was a meeting.
No one was in charge of the meeting.
Someone said 'We need more conscious control.'
'No, less.'
I felt contentious but said little.
There was no music or flowers, and the colour of the meeting was brown.
Neil lay with his head on the floor.
Under it was my jacket, rolled up.
I removed the jacket and put a waste-paper basket over his head.
There was a meeting.
Someone said that something I had said
Was very reasonable.
'If Franz had not lived, it would be necessary to invent him.'
I handed my daughter a cake a friend had brought.
She said it was useless and she had brought a bigger one.
There was a meeting.
Beryl came and said to me 'Can you manage a canoe?'
I said 'Yes'.
She said 'Oh good!' radiantly. 'Then you can take us all out
On the Regent's Canal.'
We made no progress.
Somebody paid me a dull compliment.
Someone said 'There is no news from the Kingdom of Nails'.

One or two were reading books.
Franz ... or was it 'France'?
In dreams there is no boredom.
'We need to widen the spectrum of communication.'
'Here is a poem,' said Geoffrey, standing up with an
    open book in his hand,
'Which I think will move right into the language.'

No one was listening, and he did not read.
Another said 'Everything I have not willed is boring'
    and left the room abruptly.
Stephen said
'Every concern gets the Ian Hamilton it deserves.'
You can know in a dream that you are dreaming
But outside a dream you can never be certain you are not.

A SONATA BY HANDEL

I cranked my clockwork gramophone;
The music told me I should never tire
To hear its timeless tone.
It did not tell me and I did not care
What else might chance.
Older by thirty years and more,
I hear a different fiddle dance
And different fingers press the keys
To that consummate score.
All that was seen and unforeseen –
Wife, children, sickness, death and war,
The headlines of the time between –
Whatever it has taught, has taught me nothing
More than I knew before
Of that slow, rapid, rueful and euphoric dance
The periwigged blind German first performed
Than that it once was right, is right, and will be right
Whenever sounds excite
Whatever mind, whatever years elapse:
Such music is a view of life perhaps?

FACES AT THE BRINK

Suppose, against the darkness of your mind
Just at the brink of sleep you see, as I do,
Faces and forms of people glittering small:
Malignant, threatening, or merely odd
And always enigmatic, always strangers.
What is the sense and origin, you ask,
Of such involuntary apparitions?
They lurk, they question, they accuse, they smile;
And I believe that they are those we saw
Subliminally once on crowded pavements,
In theatres, railway stations, hotel bars.
The brain must register and store these masks,
Project them as we near the brink of sleep
To disconcert and vex us as we plunge.
So if a visage angular and hard
Glares at you through myopic spectacles,
Square-jawed, brow furrowed, mouth severe and chill,
Or twisted in a thin, ironic smile,
Trying to speak, trying to comprehend –
Then to your inner dark let no such visage
Add panic or despair: consider rather
That somewhere once your path converged with mine;
And that, over that gulf of unacquaintance,
I come to wish you nothing worse than sleep.

NO STRAWBERRIES FROM MR WRIGHT

On New Year's Day the New Year Honours find
No loyal Briton quite indifferent.
This one at last, we note, has got his K;
That one must face, we read with satisfaction,
The disappointment of an MBE –
Winners at the nation's prizegiving.
You and I, of course, have ceased to meditate
For many years, even in fantasy,
The dignified letter of refusal ...
                                        This year
My thoughts revert to Mr Wright.
Him, paragon of schoolmasters forty years back,
I hear preside over the History test,
Staccato and terrific,
The praise, the blame, the rich compulsory jokes;
Or on the draughty field nursing the bowling
For the big game; or on Sunday evenings
In the brown schoolroom, while the daylight died,
Great in his chair with *David Blaize*.
                                        Each June
Brought strawberry time and Mr Wright's birthday.
I see them now, prefects, pubescent cricketers,
The paragon's inner circle seated round him
At the top table, eager and superb.
Munificent at the head sits Mr Wright
Distributing the fruit, the cream, the sugar.
These special benefactions done,
The royal eye roams down the dining-room

To where the undistinguished lower orders
Feed prosily on thick bread and grey tea.
The eye detects a favoured commoner.
'Ah, Parkhouse, you don't care for strawberries? ...
You do?' The voice of conscious bounty beckons.
'Then bring the plate up.' Then another
And another gets the cherished birthday honour,
And Mr Wright is Bacchus at the board.
I never was so favoured. I wore specs,
Had an unhealthy interest in books,
And was suspected (wrongly as it happened)
Of having cheated in the sports. At twelve
I bore no malice. Philosophically
I accepted the royal will. It was my fault.
I did not hate strawberries, or Mr Wright;
I did not even hate my friends.
       And so
I wonder what has chanced in forty years
To make me hate buyers of birthday love,
And why to me all Mr Wrights are wrong.

YOU AND NOT YOU

Practise the furtive eye, the mean excuse,
The casual voice that hides the anxious lie;
Pretend to cynicism, wear a beard,
Reject all fair advances with abuse.

Then none but your true friends will recognise,
If friend remain, the decent man at last,
When newly shaven, self-revealed and free,
You stand to greet the day of undisguise.

PERSONALITY CULT

Instructions by a Celebrity for his Posthumous Radio Portrait

When I am very dead, remember me,
But not the real me: leave that alone.
Call on the raddled dowager in Venice
And prop her up before a microphone.
My tamest jokes, most threadbare platitudes
She will retail in clichés all her own:
Then let the old bar bore pontificate
About my 'characteristic attitudes'.
Exhume the gardener; he will proudly boast
Of how I spoke to him as to a gent.
Let the world know how much my friendship meant
To the quack writer whom I hated most.
But above all, the ghosts of hostesses
At Georgian weekends, long in tooth and claw,
In tones as flat as original prints
Must quaveringly tell how on their lawns
In Berkshire, or amidst the Chelsea chintz,
I chatted literature with Bonar Law.
Say I was kind to animals and tradesmen;
Say how I lisped, and how my back-hair curled;
But do not say in Gath and Askelon
You bored me once and now you bore the world.
When I am very dead, remember me;
Let anything be told except the truth.
They didn't know me; I was no one's poodle
Vice made me man in age and fear in youth.

POETRY FESTIVAL

Wrapped in my enigmatic small cigar
I register the world of noise
Where every poet is a megaphone
Which shouts immortal megaphone.
Trumpet narcissus is a flower
Of which the simple message is itself
And trifling indications show
It does not have the trick of human love.
The inventor's scientific care
Could if it would provide the antidote,
Patent a small effectual cigar
To emanate a soundproof smoke.

ON TWO POETS

competing with each other as to which preaches in the more churches.

Mistrust, young man, the protestants of your age,
Rebels beneath the banners of dissent:
You'll live to see them man no barricades
But climb the pulpits of the establishment.

THE BATTLE OF LEWES: 14 MAY 1264

Crows on the downland elms observe the triumph
Of sword and arrow upon flesh and bone.
Harsh and ironical their evening chorus
Over the meadows where the dying moan.

Victor and vanquished both no doubt were right;
Both called upon the Bringer of All Good
To aid the cause of Simon or the King.
Which makes the Ouse redder with his blood?

Did they achieve this brotherhood of death
That the hired clerk might scratch upon his page
'Now England breathes in hope of liberty'?
Was it for this strife of pride and rage?

So in the Priory they patch a peace,
And fatalistic monks bury the dead;
In the low houses sob the fatherless,
While 'Caw caw' rasp the sceptics overhead.

Now England breathes in hope of liberty!
So let us ask the Bringer of All Good,
How many more do his intents require
That in red Ouse they find their brotherhood?

from
Poems and Paraphrases
(1972)

ROUGH WEATHER

To share with you this rough, divisive weather
And not to grieve because we have to share it,
Desire to wear the dark of night together
And feel no colder that we do not wear it,
Because sometimes my sight of you is clearer,
The memory not clouded by the sense,
To know that nothing now can make you dearer
Than does the close touch of intelligence,
To be the prisoner of your kindnesses
And tell myself I want you to be free,
To wish you here with me despite all this,
To wish you here, knowing you cannot be –
This is a way of love in our rough season,
This side of madness, the other side of reason.

NOT TO BE GREEDY

Not to be greedy for you, not to hoard you;
Not to begrudge you others to whom also
You have much to give;
Not to repine at absence, imagine neglect;
Not to be jealous, envious; still less to gorge
On the self-loving sweets of gratitude,
The masochistic bread of self-abasement,
The secret hope that you will never be free,
Despite the freedom fiercely exchanged between us –
All this is hard. To be an ideal
Is to be hard. To be hard is an ideal.

THE SPARK

If, as you read, you sigh and yawn,
Remember, I am one who talks
And thinks and writes and does not live.
So if I say I live in you,
Do not retort I overstate:
I reverence him, I warm to her,
I love them but they do not feed
The fire by which I almost live.

The fire by which I almost live
Was once a blaze, is now a spark,
So if you sigh and yawn, that spark
Will glow the more because you breathe.

LATE LOVE

If of this man you know the history,
Secret and innermost, then you know well
That of the four loves of his proper being
Yours is the latest and perhaps the last.
Sounds we are born to and survive our age
Are those the wind makes, blowing round the world,
To which we add, 'I want, I wish, I love'.
We give the cosmic breath significance.

SEPTEMBER DUSK

The girl and the five boys have gone with their
    burden of apples,
A tangle of bright clothes and disputation.
Darkness spreads from under the leaves of the fig-tree,
The brown nut-tree and the bramble thicket.
The territorial birds have stationed themselves
    for the night;
Some talk – none sings. There can be too much silence.
And too much certainty, as that your light tread
Will not disturb this gloom, your voice this silence.
In mockery perhaps it might be asking
'What is a thousand miles to one who hears?'
And I might answer,
    'Simplest things are hardest to accept.
Distance is simple. Causes of grief are many,
    but all simple.'
Children and birds have closed the book of day,
But I shall turn the pages of the night
Lying with my erosive enemy
Far from the echo of a voice, a footfall.

MESSAGE

Be absolute for poetry, my friend,
Or your insatiate spirit will go hungry,
Knocking on deaf men's doors to ask for bread.
Who has the saving word will never starve.
There was a wave of bitterness on which
I swam ashore. Naked, companionless,
I had exactly life and nothing more.
The fates gave us a choice of this or that.
There is no bargaining. It was either death
Or life upon this salty element,
Banged from one desperate corner to the next,
The taste of salt for ever on my tongue.

THE CHILDREN

These pretty children with their reading eyes
Distract you from the journey and the prize.
It is a chaste, an innocent distraction;
Of you they make this innocent exaction,
That you take note of them, and smile, and look,
And be at once their mirror and their book.
They need it so, and you desire it so;
And through your voice in time they come to know
The essential difference of their condition,
Demanding as their right its recognition.
The courting tone is now their expectation,
Monarch and subject each in his own station.
And if they harden, they will feel no shame;
For their corruption you must take the blame.
Their watching eyes will read, as due, your guilt,
On which, and not on their mere pride, is built
The boundless bounty of their self-regard.
Necessities of self-defence are hard.
Pursue the journey; suffer to be wise,
And win the loser's consolation prize.

FIN DE SAISON

Much of my life – how much? – has been transacted
At café counters on the sunny streets:
But now evening descends, the leaves descend,
And yawning waiters hurry on my death.
It is ordained no man shall have for long
The faculty of self-regeneration,
So with a syllable of leave-taking,
A final tip, I drift into the night.
Next week the cafés close for renovation.

ANIMULA

No one knows, no one cares –
An old soul
In a narrow cottage,
A parlour,
A kitchen,
And upstairs
A narrow bedroom,
A narrow bed –
A particle of immemorial life.

from
The Closed Door
(1977)

MADRIGAL

Love me and walk.
Your animal tread beside me
Transforms the sterile stone to springing pasture
Where goatfoot gods might prance.
Love me or not – but walk,
So that a cripple might be moved to dance.

Love me and smile.
A sly Giaconda gleam
Irradiates the world's enclouded leagues,
My world of grief and greed.
Love me or not – but smile:
The human comedy is all we need.

Love me and speak.
Your eloquent voice could change
A politician's cant to holy writ,
A charlatan's boast to truth.
Love me or not – but speak
To ageing ears the honest lies of youth.

THE CLOSED DOOR

After the candour and the commonplaces,
The traffic of expiring voices,
After the door has closed,
Steps that stalk the empty room are yours
And yours the words that fill the silences.
Your face is the obsessive tune
That someone some day will recover
Out of the manuscripts of time
When I no longer am your lover,
Your steps the bass, your smile the melody
When night has closed the door.
'Unloving Kindness' they will name
This unassuming air.

THE MARRIAGE OF FIGARO

Precise and mathematical as music,
Snowflakes compile the everlasting snow
Which we call Mozart's *Figaro*.

The tale is of an average sensual man –
A valet and a maid resolved on marriage,
Worldy-mature and cunning in contrivance
Against the Count-philanderer and their ruin.
Pride, jealousy, expiring feudal powers,
Lust's ageing bored compulsion – these possess him.
His Countess mourns: 'Where now are the tender hours?'
Angelic song alone is left her
Whose heart is never dead but ever dying.
A page-boy, crazed by first infatuation,
Finds his new-budded world in nature's sighing.
'What thing is love?' he breathes, and in his need
He cannot guess it is kind of death,
And in the pulsing fervour of young passion
Is not to know it ends in spite and greed:
The valet's parents show us love's fourth age.

All now is finished. Starlit night
Irradiates the trackless peaks of snow.
All is extinguished on the darkened stage.
Two centuries ago
They acted out the human puppet-show.
When we reanimate the scene
It is the music lives and triumphs,

Obliterating all except itself.
This music, like compassionate snow,
Perpetuates the human show,
Touching the circle of the timeless stars.

THE ACT OF DEATH

The act of death was too extreme
To tell me what you could not say.
There must have been a gentler way.
I plant my sorrow in your garden,
And every hanging flower weeps
Because you are not here to care.
There must have been a gentler way.
They hang their heads in dumb despair
Because you are not here to care.
I plant my sorrow in your garden:
Up spring the seeds. The weeds encroach
To deprecate my cry for pardon.
There must have been a gentler way
Than that extreme, that last reproach.
You dead, have you become the fate
Inexorable, insatiate,
That will not let me expiate
The wrong, the loss, the love, the hate
That ended in the act of death.

REFERENCES

Poetic Works by James Reeves

Experiment. A magazine of poetry and prose. Edited by Jacob Bronowski and Hugh Sykes (Cambridge: Trinity College, 1928-1931)

Songs for Sixpence. A series of single new poems by young Cambridge poets. Edited by Jacob Bronowski and James Reeves (Cambridge: W. Heffer & Sons, 1929)

The Natural Need (London: Constable & Co, 1935)

The Imprisoned Sea (London: Editions Poetry, 1949)

The Password (London: Heinemann, 1952)

The Talking Skull (London: Heinemann, 1958)

Collected Poems 1929-1959 (London: Heinemann, 1960)

The Questioning Tiger (London: Heinemann, 1964)

Subsong (London: Heinemann, 1969)

Poems and Paraphrases (London: Heinemann, 1972)

Collected Poems 1929-1974 (London: Heinemann, 1974)

The Closed Door (Sidcot: Gruffyground Press, 1977)

Other Works by James Reeves Cited in the Introduction

Chaucer. Lyric and Allegory (London: Heinemann Educational, 1970)

Complete Poems for Children (London: Faber and Faber, 2009)

The Everlasting Circle. English traditional verse from the manuscripts of S. Baring-Gould, H.E.D. Hammond and George B. Gardiner (London: Heinemann, 1960)

Georgian Poetry. Selected and Introduced by James Reeves (Harmondsworth: Penguin Books, 1962)

The Idiom of the People. English traditional verse from the manuscripts of C.J. Sharp (London: Heinemann, 1958)

'Introduction' to *Collected Poems of James Reeves 1929-1959* (London: Heinemann, 1960) pp11-16)

Selected Poems of Gerard Manley Hopkins (London: Heinemann, 1953)

Selected Poems of John Clare (London: Heinemann, 1958)

Selected Poems of John Donne (London: Heinemann, 1967)

Teaching Poetry (London: Heinemann, 1958)

The Critical Sense (London: Heinemann, 1956)

The Poets' World. An Anthology of English Poetry (London: Heinemann, 1948)

Understanding Poetry (London: Heinemann, 1948)

Other Works Cited

Cary Archard (Ed). *Alun Lewis: Collected Poems* (Cardiff: Seren Press, 2007)

Peter Davies (Ed). *Martin Seymour-Smith: Collected Poems 1943-1993* (London: Greenwich Exchange Press, 2004)

Ian Hamilton (Ed). *The Oxford Companion to Twentieth Century Poetry in English* (Oxford: Oxford University Press, 1996)

Warren Hope and Jonathan Barker (Eds). *Norman Cameron: Collected Poems and Selected Translations* (London: Anvil Press, 2011)

Robert Nye (Ed). *Some Poems by James Reeves* (Warwick: Greville Press, 2009)

Paul O'Prey (Ed). *In Broken Images. Selected Letters of Robert Graves 1914-1946* (London: Hutchinson, 1982)

Dimitrios Politis. 'Intertextuality in James Reeves verses for children' in *International Journal of English and Literature* (2012) Volume 3, Number 3, pp. 55-59.

Peter Scupham. 'James Reeves' in *PN Review* (2000) Volume 27, Issue 1, pp. 40-42.

Miranda Seymour. *Robert Graves. A Life on the Edge* (London: Doubleday, 1995)

A NOTE ON THE TEXT

Most of Reeves' previously published poems appeared in *Collected Poems 1929-1974*. When compiling it, Reeves very occasionally changed titles and made small changes to the texts. Working on the assumption that it is the final version of a poem which should stand, in all cases it is the versions from this later collection which are included here. The *Collected* however was not definitive and Reeves omitted around sixty poems, mostly from *The Natural Need* and *The Password*, whilst it also could not include any of the eight poems published in the small pamphlet, *The Closed Door* (1977). These poems have been incorporated into the appropriate places throughout.

AUTHOR'S ACKNOWLEDGMENTS

My thanks go to archivists Charlie Clare at Stowe School and Katy Green at Jesus College, Cambridge both of whom provided useful information on Reeves' school and university days. In addition, John Kay of the Lewes History Society kindly fielded queries about Reeves' last years in Lewes. My biggest thanks however must go to Gareth Reeves, James' son and also himself an exceptional poet, who took a lot of time over email to discuss his father with me and provided much helpful information and suggestion as well as signposting a number of his own poems which deal directly with his family relationships.

INDEX OF TITLES

'A Letter to Posterity' *79*

'And So They Came to Live at Daffodil Water' *85*

A Fire I Lit *68*

A Matter of Discipline *57*

A Note on the Text

A Sonata by Handel *121*

A Sonnet in Winter *73*

A Stoical Robin *96*

A Violin Concerto *62*

Aeons Hence *52*

All Days but One *115*

An Academic *88*

Animula *141*

At the Window *39*

Bestiary *47*

Bruges *102*

Counsel to Boys *78*

De Fesch *95*

Demigods *100*

Discharged from Hospital *98*

Evolution of a Painter *93*

Faces at the Brink *122*

Fin De Saison *140*

For Years We Traced *54*

Fragments of a Landscape *71*

Generation of a Critic *101*

Goat and Compasses *110*

Grand Opera *112*

Greenhallows *49*

Had I Passion to Match my Skill *63*

Hartland Quay *37*

Homage to the Moth *89*

Important Insects *94*

Improvisations *107*
In the Clubhouse *66*
In the Train *65*
Indirect Speech *109*

Late Love *136*
Leaving Town *64*

Madrigal *145*
Message *138*
Metamorphosis *118*
Misgivings *48*
Music in the Wood *53*

No Strawberries from Mr Wright *123*
No Tears for Miss Macassar *99*
Not To Be Greedy *134*
Novels I Have Never Written *74*

Old Crabbed Men *70*
On a Poet *86*
On Two Poets *128*

Personality Cult *126*
Planning Permission *104*
Poet of Birds *80*
Poetry Festival *127*
Poor Woman *106*

Repose *38*
Rough Weather *133*

September Dusk *137*
Song (The Sleep I Lost) *117*

The Act of Death *149*
The Battle of Lewes: 14 May 1264 *129*
The Children *139*
The Closed Door *146*
The Conspirators 1940 *46*
The Dancers *45*
The Infernal Machine *76*
The Little Brother *69*
The Marriage of Figaro *147*
The Meeting *119*
The Prisoners *67*
The Solvers *111*

The Spark *135*

The Stone Gentleman *77*

The Talk *87*

The Tiger *103*

The Tree of Life *61*

This Corrupt Music *116*

This Mood of Murder *84*

Thoughts and Memories *41*

Thoughts Indoors *56*

To Norman Cameron 1905-1953 *83*

Two Minds *55*

Vulture Absence *72*

Winter Speculation *40*

You and Not You *125*